Old Hertfordshire R

by

Catherine Rothwell

Published by Richard Netherwood Ltd, Fulstone Barn, New Mill, Huddersfield, West Yorkshire
Text © Catherine Rothwell 1991
Printed in Yugoslavia by Gorenjski Tisk P.O.

Gorhambury Park was built between 1563 and 1568, up hill from the old manor house, just one example from a great wave of country-house building, and although a simple, single courtyard house, the expenditure of its owner, Sir Nicholas Bacon, was phenomenal. His motto, "Mediocria Firma", was inscribed on all the tiles and the chimney piece. Sir Francis Bacon who followed added a second courtyard and built a completely new house in the valley near the Ver, which cost £10,000, his ways being no less lavish. "None of his servants durst appeare before him without Spanish leather boots, for he would smell the neates (ox) leather which offended him." By the 1770s the brickwork of Gorhambury House was so bad it had to be abandoned. The present House was built in the late 1770s with a grand Corinthian portico. This photograph of the ruins of Sir Francis Bacon's house was taken in the 1920s.

Introduction

The traveller in Hertfordshire is indeed a traveller in time. Londoners' playground, administratively created in Saxon days and commuter country ever since, in its county town of Hertford, that gathering place of rivers, was held the very first Synod of the Church of England. Here too was Richard 11 deposed and from here Charles 1 set out on a course which cost him his throne. The bells of Braughing and Flaunden rang out the news that the Spanish Armada had been utterly routed. But long before that, Romans, Saxons and Normans marched through. Here are the trade routes of the Ancient Britons, an area ringing with the names of great Roman roads: Ermine; Stane; Akeman; Watling Street; and that favourite from my youth, the Icknield Way.

Brilliant plans and inventions came from Hertfordshire. Under the guidance of Sir Hugh Myddleton, banker and goldsmith, clear chalk springs supplied London with water from land close to the Chilterns. His 17th. century invention was called the New River Scheme. "Chalking from pits", an old method by which chalk was dug from subsoil and spread on land, produced an almost permanent improvement in the soil.

Land values have always been high because of proximity to the capital and subsequent demand from influential people, some with a high place in history, for example, courtiers from the days of the first Elizabeth, herself reared in the county, as was her dour half sister, Mary Tudor.

Old Coaching Inns in leafy villages are reminders of the days when 2 hours 3 minutes, and no more, was scheduled for the 22 1/2 miles to St. Alban's from the Peacock, Islington. The "Wonder" coach left at 6.45 a.m. to arrive almost invariably outside Mr. Sherman's establishment at 8.48 a.m.. It is interesting also to look back on prices that were current in the days of these old recipes. The steam yacht "Ceylon" on August 6th. 1884 left Gravesend to take passengers on a fortnight's cruise round the United Kingdom for £25, two in a cabin. A Dalmaine Piano could be purchased for £10, 6 Eureka shirts, post free to your door, 40 shillings, and a pound of Chingwo tea cost only one shilling and eightpence.

Perhaps even more remarkable were advertisements for Epp's and Fry's Cocoa, Borwick's Baking Powder and Bird's Custard Powder, the latter making a great splash in The Graphic: "Richest custard without eggs! A great luxury! The original and only genuine, in six-penny boxes, sufficient for 3 pints." In the days when it was not unusual, with weekend guests in mind, for Hertfordshire country houses to order 12 dozen eggs and a gallon of cream, such new-found convenience was bound to be trumpeted forth.

Food in Britain was renowned in the 18th and early 19th centuries, the envy of Europe whose ambassadors and rich visitors enthusiastically reported upon it. In a time of both quality and quantity, even country people ate better than their counterparts abroad. Traditional English cookery then relied on the superb quality of its veal, lamb, beef, wild game birds, hares, rabbits, sea and river fish. Travellers' tales veered towards the abundance of oysters which the English used with amazing profligacy until stocks became scarce. The Romans loved them. Many oyster shells were found at the Roman villa razed by the Iceni, near Royston.

The freshness of our vegetables, currants, plum, apples, the excellence of bread made from stone-ground corn, and the home-brewed ale provided at Coaching Inns were all topics. There also existed a large variety of sauces, none of which needed to fall back on strong flavours for disguising poor food, sauces which were used to complement for example, succulent lamb which grazed on chalk, thyme-clad uplands.

Nowadays we have to search diligently for that quality taken for granted before mass-produced and packaged food arrived, but interest in quality has of late strongly revived. As traditional cook Ruth Mott recently said in her television series, "The end product can only be as good as the ingredients put into it."

That decline in cooking which took away an enviable reputation was due to both lack of interest and changed domestic circumstances, but Hertfordshire, catering long for distinguished and discerning people, must always have sustained traditional hospitality. An amazing panoply of famous names is linked with the county: Charles Dickens; George Bernard Shaw; Apsley Cherry Gerrard; George Orwell; E.M. Forster; Cecil Rhodes; Cardinal Manning; George Chapman; Thomas Hearne; Henry Bessemer; Nicholas Breakspear; Beatrix Potter; Lord Cecil; Sir Francis Bacon and others. Even the entire British Parliament on two occasions when the Great Plague was raging decamped to Hertfordshire.

Under much humbler circumstances I first rode over the Hertfordshire borderin the early 1940s on a second-hand bicycle costing £3. It never crossed my mind that old postcards of St. Alban's from an album spotted on a market stall at Watford on one visit would some fifty years later help to illustrate a little cookery book. Inside the album was a 1932 report on the Verulamium Excavation Committee, signed by C.E. Jones of Warners Russell Avenue, St. Alban's."... A sum of £1,200 is required. You are asked to send donations large and small." The fruits of a traveller in time! Such history, and all for ten shillings in the days of old money!

Of many descriptions: "hearty, homely, loving Hertfordshire"; "the green plains"; or E.M. Forster's "gently pastoral, England at its quietest"; all of which are true, as I have grown to know the county better I feel that the Travel Trade Manual's up-to-the-minute description is most apt. People hurtle through "England's best kept secret" on Euston-bound Pullman Expresses with scarcely a glance beyond the Ovaltine girl, idly noting pleasant rurality, undulating woods, rivers and canal. I did so myself for many years, but returning to Hertfordshire as a pensioner, with time to stand and stare, to talk to people, to explore, has been both rare treat and surprise.

Collecting old recipes long-relished by Hertfordshire natives in this richly endowed county of more than 100 parks, backed also with hindsight from having scoured so many other counties, we discovered a great awareness of traditional dishes based on quality.

As we left the City on one of our last visits, thankfully escaping the hell of Hangar Lane traffic and making for that most dramatic coup d'oeil, the Chiltern Gap, where suddenly miles of countryside roll into view, we could well understand the feelings of Charles Lamb who loved Hertfordshire. Seeking the peace of Mackery End, the 16th century farmhouse near Wheathampstead, he was regularly "turning his back on the detested walls". It was with a sense of relief that we too sped into Hertfordshire, sure of a good meal and a comfortable bed. In our travels we had heard: "Us allus tells folk Suffolk's flat - helps keep they furriners out." To remain England's best kept secret, perhaps Hertfordshire has a similar "recipe".

Catherine Rothwell

Old Country Remedies

To relieve a bruise take one handful of chamomile flowers or elder flowers

1/2 pint vinegar
1/4 pint brandy

Boil the flowers in a pint of water. Strain into jug. Add vinegar and brandy. To be applied as hot as the sufferer can bear.

A potato poultice was thought to give relief from sunburn. It was made from grated raw potato spread between gauze and applied to the burn.

To soothe unbroken chilblains boil 9 ounces of celery stalks in 2 pints of water. When cool, dip the hands or feet in the pitcher.

Fig leaves boiled with honey were a remedy for coughs and colds.

To remove a wart, rub with radish juice twice a day.

A few leaves of sage or a pinch of aniseed in a cup of boiling water will relieve indigestion.

To cure insomnia, use a pillow filled with hops (Hertfordshire held hop fairs).

To relieve pleurisy, apply leeks cooked in a cabbage leaf.

Rosemary leaves soaked in wine were used to soothe bee or wasp stings. Long ago there was a belief in Hertfordshire that headaches could be charmed away by touching a rope that had been used for a public hanging.

A Hertfordshire Cold Remedy

6 lemons	4 oranges
1/4 lb seedless raisins	3 cups Hertfordshire honey
3 oz ginger	1 gallon water

Wash the lemons and oranges and squeeze out their juice. Add the other ingredients to the water in a large pan and bring to the boil then simmer for one hour. Skim. When cool, add the fruit juice. Pour into a pitcher and leave overnight. The dose was 2 cups a day.

Cough Medicine

This remedy is over 200 years old. Shred a handful of rosemary. Pour boiling water onto it and leave it to stand covered on the hob or by the fire. Next day strain the liquid, adding 1 lb of sugar to each half pint of the rosemary water. Boil until the mixture becomes syrupy. A very soothing, pleasant drink.

Violet vinegar and syrup of violets could not be made today unless you had your own violet banks or mossy wood. The nature warden would frown, but old country recipes recommended for remedying ailments are still of interest.

Violet vinegar was made by boiling white vinegar with half a jar of violets (enough vinegar to fill the jar). When cold, the liquid was strained and bottled.

Extraordinary Large

Twelfth Cake,

18 FEET IN CIRCUMFERENCE,

TO BE SEEN AT

ADAMS's, 41, Cheapside,

OPPOSITE WOOD STREET.

This Cake considerably surpasses in size any that has hitherto been made in London, or, in fact, in the world: its weight is nearly Half a Ton, and actually contains Two Hundred and a Half weight of Currants, and upwards of ONE THOUSAND EGGS.

This Wonderful Cake is ready for Public inspection, as above, where orders for any part will be received, and duly attended to.

N.B.—Cake packed for any art of the United Kingdom.

Jan. 3, 1811.

Syrup of Violets was considered very good for sore throats.

Soak 2 lb of violets in 3 pints of water for 24 hours. Keep covered. Strain off the liquor and add sugar to it in proportion of 1 lb to 1 pint. Stir until the sugar dissolves. The liquor was brought to the boil slowly and bottled when cold.

Forty years ago I heard of a room being filled with violets to succour a patient terminally ill with cancer.

A favourite picnic drink of the Edwardians was claret cup with borage leaves floating on top.

When Anneka Rice dropped in at Hatfield Palace on one of her Treasure Hunts she was presented with a jar of Heavy Mead which contains lots of honey.

Barbara Cartland, world-famous novelist and great believer in the use of honey, who lives in Hertfordshire, wrote to us: "Mead in some form has been brewed by primitive tribes all over the world from India to Lithuania and always contained honey. Ancient Greeks called their honey wine Hydromel and believed it would disperse anger, sweep away sadness and affliction of the mind and make those who drink it, warm and lovely. This is why honey has always been called 'The Food of Love'."

Some of this Twelfth Cake would undoubtedly reach Hertfordshire. Baked for the year 1811, these cakes had a long history behind them and were eaten on old Christmas Day, before rearrangement of the calendar in 1752 took place. This rich, plum cake on show at 41 Cheapside, London, contained 1,000 eggs and weighed half a ton. The Romans were said to eat a twelfth cake at their Saturnalia, so these cakes are truly pagan. Adam's at Cheapside were close to Bread Street, at one time the chief bread market in the City, "a street of divers fair inns, inhabited by rich merchants". John Milton was born there.

We were delighted to receive the following recipe from Hertford-shire novelist and health expert Barbara Cartland.

Chicken, Honey and Oranges

1 3lb chicken	1/2 cup butter
1/4 cup flour	1 teaspoon salt
2 teaspoons paprika	2 tablespoons honey
1/2 teaspoon ginger	1 1/2 cups orange juice
1 1/2 cups water	1 teaspoon tabasco sauce
2 oranges	1/4 teaspoon pepper

Sprinkle chicken with salt, pepper, paprika and brown in butter. Remove chicken and stir into the casserole the flour, honey, tabasco, ginger, orange juice and water. Return chicken to the sauce, cover and cook until chicken is tender. Slice oranges 1/2 inch thick and add to chicken. Cook for a short while longer then serve.

Chef Nigel Gordon added: "This is a very unusual dish and the orange gives it a very nice flavour."

This handsome church at Cheshunt amongst fine chestnut trees was begun in 1418 by its Rector Nicholas Dixon whose brass inscription is below the altar table; it took 30 years to complete. It possesses a huge, armoured coffer with three locks, the church chest for 400 years, and an old barrel organ having 10 tunes on each barrel. By the altar is the tomb of the Dacres family, Robert Dacres, the first named, being Privy Councillor to Henry VIII.

Regina Refresher

1/2 glass fresh orange juice	ice
1/2 glass Perrier water	10 cc Regina Royal
dash of grenadine	Concorde Jelly

Put the ice, orange juice, Perrier and Concorde into a small tumbler ("Slim Jim") and stir with a cocktail stirrer. Add the grenadine and serve.

This can hardly be called an old recipe but its basis, goes back to mediaeval days when honey was served as sweetener in many dishes. A recipe provided by the Hertfordshire Company, Regina Royal Jelly Ltd.

Honey Salad Dressing

2 tablespoons Hertfordshire honey	a little garlic
ground black pepper and sea salt	2 tablespoons salad oil
	2 tablespoons lemon juice

Whisk all together and place in a cool larder. Use after 30 minutes.

A very good tip to get the last drop of juice out of a lemon before squeezing it is to roll it vigorously on a hard surface, pressing hard, then plunge it in very hot water for a few seconds. Lemon juice sprinkled on strawberries improves their flavour, as it does that of mushrooms.

Faggots of herbs were used to sweeten the hives of bees when they were being cleaned out, the scent of herbs not being offensive to bees.

As in other counties a century ago most cottagers kept a pig, despatched at the appointed time by the owner or an itinerant pig killer. The pig was laid on a timbrel and its blood, kept constantly stirred, drained into a bowl to make black puddings. Brawn and spare ribs were considered to be very tasty and were handed to neighbours who in turn contributed their "home-killed" when the time came. One family could not cope with all the trimmings when there was no means of freezing meat. Smoking, curing and salting made joints last longer, but in the countryside there were reported cases of poisoning from bad pork.

William Cobbett in 1822 gave good advice: "To kill a pig nicely is so much a profession it is better to pay a shilling for having it done .... Hang bacon in the chimney where no rain can drip on it, smoking over a wood fire kept constantly burning for one month."

He loved Hertfordshire farmhouses and in his "Cottage Economy" wrote: "The grass which I got in Hertfordshire, than which I think nothing can be more beautiful, was cut when the wheat was in full bloom." He recommended mustard to go with the fat bacon and black puddings, adding, "Why buy this when you can grow it in your own garden?"

Cobbett was very interested in English straw plait for the making of hats and bonnets which helped to keep Hertfordshire villages prosperous.

Rabbit and Onion Bake

Arrange a jointed rabbit in a baking tin, mixing with it crumbled, stale bread. Season all with pepper, salt and mixed herbs. Arrange 3 rashers of bacon over this and when you have ready 1/2 lb par-boiled onions, pour these, with the onion water, gently over the rabbit etc. Bake in a moderate oven for 1 1/2 hours, basting at frequent intervals.

Pork could be substituted for rabbit. The importance of the pig and its widespread use in old recipes is instanced by mention in a 17th century Hertfordshire will which left amongst bequests: "... one quarter of the hogg now a 'fatting in the yard, when he is killed."

Devilled Kidneys

Clean, core and slit the kidneys. Dip in melted butter, lay flat and grill for about 5 minutes. Sprinkled with lemon juice, chopped parsley and what was called Devil Butter (butter mixed with curry paste), these were introduced to London friends of my Uncle Willie up from the country when he became a Borough Treasurer. As children, visiting his Herne Hill villa, we were served them on toast as a great breakfast treat by his housekeeper Miss Robertson, but minus the Devil Butter.

Devilling, a forgotten technique, was popular in Hertfordshire in the 19th century, provoking thirst amongst gentlemen, for whom it was recommended at their clubs. Anchovy paste mixed with curry powder, cayenne pepper and mustard was spread on hot biscuits and served on snowy napkins. Jars of devilled pepper were part of a cook's armoury. Alexis Soyer, famous chef who organised Field Kitchens for the British army during the Crimean War, called it "a Mephistophelian process".

The 300 years old Fox and Hounds at Barley has this unusual inn sign : hounds and huntsmen pursuing a fox. These painted figures on a beam spanning the whole road were photographed in the 1930s. Barley has an old wooden lock-up, a smithy and a Tudor town hall amongst a wealth of old houses and cottages.

The waterfall at Hoddesden was photographed in the 1930s. Izaac Walton of "Compleat Angler" fame fished the River Lea, his favourite Hoddesden inn being the Thatched House. The River Lea waters the moat of what is left of old Rye House a mile away. This remnant consists of a 16th century gatehouse which used to house the 'Great Bed of Ware', but which is mainly associated with the Rye House Plot, an attempt in 1683 to assassinate Charles 11 and his brother James. Hoddesden's focal point is the clock tower beneath which a market dating from the 13th century is held.

Pork Plugger

This word of mouth recipe, exchanged on a Hertfordshire High Street, is very tasty and, I am told, has been a favourite for years. Equal quantities of chopped bacon and onion are mixed together. Make an oblong of suet crust by mixing 8 oz flour, 4 oz suet and a little water and roll to about 1/2 inch thickness. Spread the filling of bacon and onion, bound with a little water and well-peppered, onto the suet pastry. Scatter a good tablespoon of sage on top, roll up, tie in a floured cloth and steam for 2 1/2 hours. Carrots and turnips are served with it and sprigs of parsley, which are meant to be eaten, not regarded as mere decoration!

Clangers

are very similar, made from recipes which have been used for a long time in Hertfordshire. Clanger-eating contests have been held near Hemel Hempstead.

8 oz flour	4 oz suet (grated)
8 oz lean bacon	1 large Spanish onion
parsley and sage	

Remove rind from bacon and chop it finely. Peel onion and chop this finely. Mix the suet pastry, binding it with a little water. Line a greased pudding basin. Place the bacon in a frying pan over low heat to get the fat running. Fry the chopped onion until golden-brown and mix with the bacon. Sprinkle with fresh, chopped parsley, sage and pepper. Mix all this together and put into the basin, making a lid of suet pastry. Cover well with greaseproof paper and steam for 3 hours. Serve with chopped Spring cabbage and sliced tomatoes.

Brawn

Brawn, a classic, mediaeval food, was served with mustard and Malmsey wine or the sweetest of Madeiras. Served at Gorhambury and quite possibly at Hatfield House to the young girl who was to become Elizabeth 1.

The secret of flavour lies in long simmering. Whole pigs' heads were boiled. A more convenient but still old method is as follows:

1/2 lb shin beef   1 cow heel
1/2 lb ham or oxtail

Cover with water. Cook for 4 hours, simmering slowly, adding 2 small chopped onions, a bunch of herbs, 4 cloves, 4 peppercorns, 2 bay leaves (the last four items tied in muslin). Allow to cool. Remove meat from bones and place in a mould or pudding basin. Strain the stock over the meat and leave on a cold pantry shelf to set.

This brawn is delicious accompanied with the freshest, crunchiest green salad, and the wine of course. Malmsey wine is mentioned as early as 1478 when the Duke of Clarence was said to have drowned in a butt of Malmsey wine in the Tower. An Act of Henry VIII's reign forbade it to be sold for more than 12 pence a gallon.

The four-storeyed Clock Tower of St. Alban's is a mediaeval belfry, built in the 15th. century and restored in the 19th. The curfew bell within is even older, 600 years, and weighs a ton. It was once used to summon apprentices to work at 4 o'clock in the morning. In front, until 1702 was an Eleanor cross.

Kettle Broth

3 lb brisket beef rubbed in salt daily for three days.

Place in "kettle" or large pan with some chopped carrots, chopped onion, diced turnip and chopped leek. In the last 20 minutes of cooking, which takes about 3 hours' slow simmering, chopped, curly green cabbage is added.

Families ate the broth first, then the beef with boiled potatoes. "Any left over beef was delicious when cold."

St. Alban's was the home of the most famous of Hertfordshire witches. Mother Haggy was said to ride around the town at midday on a broomstick. She had a habit of crossing the River Ver on a kettle.

This photograph of Hatfield House was taken in 1895, the Old Palace on this site being constructed in 1496 and formerly owned by the Bishops of Ely. Henry VIII used it for his children. During Mary Tudor's reign her sister Elizabeth was kept prisoner here and was said to have been sitting under an oak tree in Hatfield Park when she heard of Mary's death and realised that she herself would become Elizabeth 1, Queen of England. Hatfield House was reported dark and desolate when in later years James II called. Everything conducive to comfort had been removed. "The only provisions left were two does on the hall table, one barrel of small beer in the cellar and a pile of faggots."

Ware Hot Cross Buns

1 lb strong white flour	1 teaspoon all spice
1/4 pint milk	2 oz butter
1 1/2 tablespoons honey	1/4 pint hot water
6 oz dried fruit (currants, raisins, peel)	1 oz fresh yeast
	1/2 teaspoon sea salt freshly ground

Melt the honey with the hot water. Add enough cold milk to make up one pint and to this smooth in the yeast. Place in a warm but not hot position. Next, rub the fat into the flour, spice, salt. Stir in the lukewarm yeast mixture and knead the dough produced. Cover and set it to rise in a warm place for 2 hours. You could meanwhile make a little pastry, which will be necessary for marking the buns with a cross.

After 2 hours, when the dough will have doubled in size by the yeast action, stir in the dried fruit and roll into 12 balls which should be gently flattened. Cut strips of pastry and place in cruciform fashion on each bun, also brushing the tops with whisked egg yolk.

Pope Ladies

St Alban's is the ancient home of this cake once sold in the shops on New Year's morning. Centuries of history and tradition must be involved. I was very interested to be told about these as my "own" north-west mediaeval market town used to bake Yule babies shaped in the figure of the Christ child from dough and placed in a "manger" or oblong pastry case containing mincemeat. These were given out at Yuletide.

Heather Fitzsimmons' recipe for Pope Ladies, which were originally distributed to the poor by the monks of St. Alban's, although their recipe was a closely guarded secret, is as follows:

1 oz fresh yeast	3/4 pint milk
1/4 lb sugar	1 1/2 lb plain flour
2 teaspoons nutmeg	1 teaspoon salt
6 oz butter	3 eggs
currants	egg and water glaze

Dissolve the yeast in the warm milk then stir in the sugar. Sift flour with nutmeg and salt. Rub in the butter. Stir in the beaten eggs and yeast, mixing well to form a soft dough. Knead the dough on a floured board. Place in a greased bowl and cover, leaving the dough to rise for one hour. Shape dough into ovals, tapering one end into a point. Use small pieces of dough to form head and arms. Make eyes with currants. Brush the Pope Ladies with beaten egg glaze. Leave to prove, then bake for 25 minutes at 190 C., 375 F., Gas mark 5.

Another Hertfordshire lady, Jean Morrison, feels the custom harks back to Roman times. Dough cakes in human form were eaten by the Romans at their Saturnalia. "Pop lady" buns, sold in St. Alban's in 1819 when Cobbett was around, were said to be "like the hot cross buns sold elsewhere on Good Friday", but they represented the Blessed Virgin Mary.

Ashwell Rich Parkin

1 lb oatmeal	1/2 lb lard
1/2 lb butter	1/4 lb sugar
2 oz ground ginger	1 lb syrup or treacle

Melt the fats together and mix with the syrup or treacle and dry ingredients, mixing all very well. Spread in greased tins and bake in a slow oven for 2 hours. When taken from the oven, mark it in portions with a knife and wait 3 days before eating. It improves with a little keeping and is an instance of the old "pound cake" principle.

King's Langley Tomato Preserve

5 lb ripe tomatoes	4 lb sugar
2 lemons	2 oz stem ginger

Peel and slice tomatoes, chop the ginger, slice the lemons and add the sugar. Cook very slowly for 3 1/2 hours until the tomato preserve is thick. Pot, seal and label.

The tomatoes are easily peeled by dropping them into boiling water which causes the skins to split.

South Country Pie

1 lb sour plums	2 lb lamb chops
2 teaspoons sugar	2 onions
1 lemon	a little brown sugar and spice

Wash and stone the plums and place in a pie dish, sprinkled with spice and sugar. Add a layer of chops and onions. Seasoning as you go, continue layering until the ingredients are all used. Finish by squeezing the lemon juice over. Place a pastry crust upon the dish and bake in a moderate oven for 1 1/2 hours.

The pastry may have originally been suet. We used a plain mix of 8 oz flour to 3 oz low cholesterol margarine, rubbed in and bound with a little water. It was necessary to cover the crust with two sheets of parchment paper, wrung out in water, to prevent over-browning.

Meesden Pudding

1 lb flour	2 oz lard
2 oz butter	2 teaspoons baking powder
3 tablespoons golden syrup	

Rub fat into flour. Warm the syrup sufficiently to make it runny and pour in. Mix well and lastly add the baking powder.

Pour into a greased basin. Cover with greaseproof paper, securing in a pudding cloth. Boil for 2 hours and serve with melted syrup.

Hertford, "capital of 150 villages and towns", stands at the meeting of three rivers and has an ancient Saxon castle for which it pays rent of half a crown a year (12 1/2p). In 673 A.D. an important meeting took place: the first national synod held by the church in this country. In Hertford lived the 17th century judge Sir Henry Chauncy who wrote The History of Hertfordshire and declared Jane Wenham to be a witch, the last woman to be sentenced. Queen Anne reprieved Jane and witchcraft was abolished from the statute book.

Almond Custard

1/4 lb almonds
yolks of 4 eggs

2 teaspoons rosewater
1 pint cream

The sweet almonds should be pounded in a mortar (nowadays ready-ground almonds can be had from supermarkets). Stir in the rosewater, then the yolks of eggs and finally the cream. Instruction continues: "Put this over a slow fire and keep it constantly stirred till it has reached its proper thickness. Pour into cups." The constant stirring is important and a double saucepan is excellent for the job.

This old recipe is typical of a score of custards with which the Victorians were familiar but which have died out. It is well worth the expense and extra trouble if you want to treat your palate.

Apple Dumplings with Burnt Cream

Allow one apple per person, cored and filled with Demerara sugar. No need to peel. Roll in shortcrust pastry to make a ball with joins at the bottom. Bake for one hour at 180 C. (We found half that time suffices in a modern oven)

Burnt Cream

Boil a pint of cream with a stick of cinnamon and some finely pared lemon peel. Take it off the heat and pour it very slowly into the yolks of 4 eggs, stirring until almost cold. Sweeten and remove the cinnamon stick and peel. Pour into a dish. When quite cold, strew white, pounded sugar over it and brown with a salamander.

This photograph of the Museum at Tring was taken in the early years of this century. Originally the private collection of the second Baron Rothschild, this museum was bequeathed to the nation in 1938. It has since become part of the British Museum of Natural History. From 1873 to 1938 Tring Park and its estate, which included a large part of the town, was the property of the Rothschild family.

Vanilla Ice Cream

This ice cream which nowadays can be placed in the refrigerator used to be prepared in "an inexpensive freezing apparatus made by taking two tins, one large and one small, and placing the smaller, packed with broken ice and freezing salt, into the larger. The ice cream was placed in the small tin, securely lidded and rolled backwards and forwards on the floor for 30 minutes, occasionally taking it up and shaking well."

1/4 pint cream	1/4 pint milk
yolk of 1 free range egg	juice of 1/2 lemon
2 tablespoons thin honey	a few drops of vanilla essence

Mix yolk of egg and honey together and add all the other ingredients. Heat in a double saucepan (or jug stood in a saucepan of hot water), stirring well all the time. Pass through a sieve and when cold, freeze.

Harpenden Strawberry Pie

1 cup flour	1/2 teaspoon salt
2 teaspoons baking powder	4 tablespoons butter
1/4 cup cold water	1 quart strawberries

Sift dry ingredients together, rub in butter very lightly with fingertips and add water slowly to make a stiff dough. Roll out on a floured board and use for bottom crust of pie, being careful to fold the paste well over the edge of the pie plate. Bake in a hot oven for 12-15 minutes. If glazed crust is desired, brush edges after baking with boiling hot syrup (2 tablespoons syrup and a tablespoon water) and return to oven for 1-2 minutes until syrup hardens. Fill the baked crust with fresh selected hulled strawberries and cover with syrup made as follows:

Add 1/2 cup sugar and 1/2 cup strawberries to 2 cups boiling water. Bring to boil and strain. Add 1 tablespoon corn starch which has been mixed with a little cold water. Cook over a hot fire for a minute or two, stirring constantly. Remove from fire and beat hard. Return to slow fire, cook very gently until thick. Pour while hot over strawberries. Serve either hot or cold.

Apple Dumplings with Hard Sauce

Peel and core 6 apples. Fill the cavity with caster sugar, sultanas and 1 clove. Using the pastry recipe for fruit pies, make enough to roll round each apple. Press the pastry together at the top with a little water. Place the apple dumplings on a buttered baking sheet, brushing the tops with yolk of egg. Bake for half an hour in a hot oven. The dumplings were brought to table, dusted with sugar, reposing in snowy-white damask napkins in silver dishes. Hard sauce was the accompaniment, made as follows:

Cream 4 oz butter and 4 oz sugar. Whip the white of an egg stiffly and mix into the creamed sugar and butter (the egg must be room temperature to avoid a curdled-looking mixture). Scatter with ground nutmeg but sparingly.

Hitchin High Street in 1916 shows the Livery and Bait stables at the Cock Hotel. A mediaeval market town, Hitchin once had a large area for an important market linked with the cottage industry of straw plaiting in the 19th. century. The work was done in the cottages and completed plaits sold to dealers in the market. Bridge Street and Tilehouse Street still have a number of old houses.

Little Gaddesden Gooseberry Pudding

4 oz grated suet	8 oz flour
6 oz gooseberries	4 oz brown sugar

Mix suet and flour together. Add the sugar, washed, topped and tailed gooseberries, mixing all well together. Put into a well-buttered basin which should be tied down with a cloth and boiled for 3 hours. Traditionally this 18th. century pudding was eaten with more sugar, but an egg custard sauce makes a good accompaniment.

Custard Mould

1 pint milk	3 eggs
1 oz caster sugar	3/4 oz gelatine
vanilla essence	

Bring the milk to almost boiling point, add sugar and well beaten eggs and stir until the mixture thickens but do not let it boil. Pour it onto the gelatine in a basin. Add a few drops of vanilla essence. Stir well until dissolved and pour into a mould or into individual glasses.

Caramel Peaches

5 peaches	1/4 pint whipped cream
1 breakfast cup brown sugar	2 tablespoons milk
1 tablespoon butter	1 tablespoon chopped nuts

Skin the peaches by dipping them into boiling water for 2 minutes. Cut in halves and remove stones. Fill the centres with whipped cream.

Join the halves together, securing with thin sticks. Place brown sugar, milk and butter in a saucepan. Stir until boiling. Simmer for 8 minutes. Beat until it begins to thicken then pour over the peaches. When cold, slide out the sticks. Top each peach with a swirl of cream and chopped almonds. These were often accompanied by sponge biscuits.

It was heart-warming to have the kindly interest of the Hertfordshire Federation of Women's Institutes, although Ida Brodersen remarked on the scarcity of old Hertfordshire recipes. One member sent the following:

Hertfordshire Rolled Beef

1 1/2 lb braising steak	2 oz grated suet
4 oz fine dry breadcrumbs	1 egg
1/2 teaspoon parsley	1/2 teaspoon sage
1/2 pint stock	salt and pepper

The steak, in one piece, was just right if 3/4 inch thick. The suet, seasoning, breadcrumbs, parsley, sage were bound with the egg and spread over the beef, which was then rolled up and tied with string. Placed in a deep pie-dish with the 1/2 pint of stock, the dish was covered and the rolled beef slowly cooked in the oven for 2 hours. After that the meat was removed and remaining liquid thickened with an ounce of flour, which was served with the meat.

Hertfordshire used to have breweries in every town but few are now left. Corn brought wealth to the county, barley being turned into malt at Bishop's Stortford, Hoddesden and Ware, "the cradle of the industry in Britain". Indeed, maltings in Hertfordshire were as common a feature of the landscape as oast houses in Kent. The photograph from 1876 shows the yard of Lucas's Brewery at Hitchin. William Lucas, a Quaker, was a man with great business flair.

Victoria Sandwich

4 oz flour	4 oz caster sugar
4 oz butter	2 eggs
1 tablespoon water	

Heat oven to 180 C. Place all ingredients in a bowl or electric mixer and beat well. Turn into 8 inch cake tin and bake for 1/2 hour. When cool, split and fill with the following jam.

Old-Fashioned Raspberry Jam

6 lb raspberries
6 lb preserving sugar

Place the fruit in a large basin over boiling water. Crush fruit with a wooden spoon. Add the hot sugar and stir until sugar is dissolved. Turn all into a preserving pan and boil for 10 minutes only. The lovely flavour of the raspberries is retained to perfection and together you have the perfect sponge cake. Queen Victoria was very fond of this cake which was made country-wide in her reign. I have come across the same recipe in a number of regions.

The photograph from Lullingstone Silk Farm, Ayot House, probably dates from the late 1930s and shows a skilled operator at her machine. Visitors can watch raw silk being produced by silk worms. Sir Lionel Lyde, owner of Ayot House in 1778, started to demolish the 14th. century church of St. Lawrence until admonished by the Bishop of Lincoln. Halting demolition, he commissioned Nicholas Reve to build a new church close by. Silk is made in Abbey Mill Lane at an 18th. century mill in St. Alban's on the site of the old Abbey Mill. Nearby is one of the smallest inns and oldest of houses in St. Alban's, built in the 16th. century on a mediaeval base, the Fighting Cocks.

Shortbread

4 oz wholemeal flour	3 oz unsalted butter
4 teaspoons brown sugar	

The oven should be heated to 180 C., 350 F., gas 4. Sift flour into the mixing bowl, setting aside the bran. Rub in the butter until the mixture resembles fine crumbs. Stir in the brown sugar. Knead the mixture into a dough, then flatten into round shape to fit into a buttered tin. Prick with a fork and just before putting in the oven, scatter the bran over the surface of the shortbread. Cook for 25 minutes. An old basic recipe for this ever-popular sweetmeat, also beloved of Queen Victoria, and which is only really delicious if made with butter.

Eel Pie

Delicious eels found in the River Gade are mentioned in the Domesday Book, a survey of England ordered by William the Conqueror.

2 lb large eels	pepper and salt fresh milled
1 large chopped Spanish onion	blade of mace
1 1/2 pints veal and chicken stock	1 oz butter
	1 dessertspoon flour
1 tablespoon lemon juice and a slice of rind	chopped parsley

Skin and clean the eels, removing head, tail and fins. Cut into two-inch lengths. Put in a pan with the finely-minced onions, lemon rind and mace. Pour over the liquid stock and simmer for 25 minutes. Put the eels in a pie dish and strain the broth, returning it to the stewpan. Thicken this with the flour blended with butter and stir in the lemon juice. When cool, pour this over the eels. Sprinkle with chopped parsley and season if necessary. When quite cold, cover with shortcrust pastry and bake for one hour in a moderate oven.

Raspberry Wine

"3 lbs raisins should be washed, stoned and cleaned thoroughly. Boil 2 gallons of spring water for 1/2 hour. Pour this boiling water over the raisins in a deep, stone jar. Add 6 quarts of fresh raspberries and 2 lb loaf sugar. Stir well and place in a cool larder. Cover. Stir it twice a day, then pass through a hair sieve, next day adding 1 lb more sugar. Put into a barrel and when fine, in about 2 months, it can be bottled."

Temple Bar at Waltham Cross is shown in this photograph from the 1920s. Designed by Sir Christopher Wren in 1672 it was erected at the Fleet Street entrance to the City of London, an earlier wooden bar having been destroyed in the Great Fire. Deemed a traffic hazard, in 1878 it was moved to Theobalds Park, having been acquired by Sir Henry Meux.

Cherry Turnovers

Cherry Turnovers were made in the days of Hertfordshire's annual Cherry fairs held at Potten End and Berkhamsted when cherries were in great profusion in the vale of Cherry Bounce. Supposedly invented by a Frithsden housewife, no specific recipe was forthcoming, but presented with a pound of luscious, stoned, washed cherries, the enterprising cook would surely make them like Coventry Godcakes, encased in squares of puff pastry, moistened at the edges and "turned over" triangle-wise after putting a little sugar and moisture with the cherries.

How to make the puff pastry:

1/2 lb fresh butter (lard, salted butter or margarine will not do)	1/2 lb white flour (dried, with a pinch of salt) cold water to mix

Rub 1 oz butter into the flour. Make a well in the centre. Squeeze in a few drops of lemon juice. Add a little water and mix to a dough which should be neither stiff nor sticky. Knead the dough until smooth and leave in a cool place. Roll out the dough 3/4 inch thick. Put the whole of the butter on it evenly in small "dabs". Fold in three and give a turn to the left. Roll out evenly. After each roll place the dough on a plate and leave in "as cold a place as possible". I was told that the butter has to be of the same consistency as the dough and that "the top of a quick oven is best for Puff Pastry".

To Prepare Rice for Curry

Half fill a clean pan with boiling water seasoned with salt. Place in the quantity of rice required. Boil quickly for 15 minutes, stirring with a clean, wooden spoon. Strain through a colander and run cold water on the rice to separate the grains. Let it drip, then after a few minutes put colander in empty stewpan and stand near the fire, turning lightly to make it free and dry. It can be served round curry or as a separate dish with meat instead of potatoes.

The meat served with rice was often in the form of mutton chops, stewed with a large onion and seasoning. Mutton was considered more wholesome than beef, especially for patients recovering from illness. If roasted, it was set before the fire and basted constantly. What was known as Roast Gigot of Mutton was cooked in an iron stewpan and needed less attention. "Two hours should cook a seven-pound leg of mutton".

Strawberry and cherry jam tends to allow the fruit to rise to the top of the pan, all fruit at the top and jelly at the bottom, so to avoid this leave the jam for about half an hour and give a good stir before finally potting. Do not, however, leave it too long. Once jam is opened, it is a good idea, especially in hot weather, to keep it at the bottom of the fridge.

The Post Office at Barley, photographed in 1900 by J. Bishop, is shown to be also the village store, selling rolls of oilcloth, hosiery, foodstuffs and baskets. Mainly the market towns served the needs of the countryside with butter, eggs, apples, mushrooms, walnuts, elderberries, bundles of herbs, young pigeons or whatever was in season, but the village shop, like the inn, was a good place to exchange gossip.

BARLEY POST OFFICE

POST OFFICE, BARLEY.

By J. Bishop

Standon Strawberry Jam

Standon Green End has a commemorative Balloon Stone, a sandstone boulder marking the spot where Vincenzo Lunardi completed the first balloon flight in England on September 15th 1784. He took his cat and his dog with him but the cat did not like it, so Vincenzo descended and carefully handed over the cat to a surprised village lady in North Mymms before rising again.

7 lb strawberries	6 lb sugar
juice of 1 lemon	

Pick the strawberries when dry and just ripe. There is no need to warm the sugar. Place the washed, drained, hulled strawberries in a preserving pan with the lemon juice. Heat gradually and simmer until fruit is soft. Add sugar to fruit and dissolve slowly, stirring all the time with a wooden spoon. Increase heat and boil rapidly until a set is reached.

Blackberry Wine

4 quarts ripe blackberries	5 quarts water
1 1/4 teaspoons fresh yeast	1 lb raisins
7 lb sugar	

Wash and pick the fruit (elderberries may be used instead of blackberries). Boil the water and pour over the fruit. Allow to cool. Add yeast. Cover and leave for a week, when it should be strained and the sugar added. Stir sugar in till all dissolved then add the raisins. Cover and leave to work for a further week. Bottle when all fermentation has ceased. It is ready for drinking in 6 months.

Blackberry Wine

"The blackberries should be just ripe and gathered on a dry day. Use a vessel with a tap fitted at the bottom. Put the fruit in this and cover with boiling water. After it has cooled, mash the berries with both hands and then let them stand covered for 4 days. Draw off the liquid into another vessel. Now, to every gallon of liquid allow 1 lb sugar, mixing well. Put it into a cask to work for 10 days, keeping the cask well filled and discarding the lees of the liquid. When it has ceased to work, bung it down. In 6 months the wine may be bottled."

Molasses Cake

All measurements are level

1/2 cup margarine	1/4 teaspoon salt
1/2 cup molasses	1/2 cup brown sugar
2 cups flour	1 egg
1/4 teaspoon bicarb of soda	3 teaspoons baking powder
1 teaspoon cinnamon	1/2 teaspoon allspice
	1/2 cup milk

Cream the margarine, adding sugar slowly and beating continuously. Add beaten egg and molasses (syrup or treacle). Add half of the flour, with baking powder, salt, soda and spices sifted together. Add milk and rest of dry ingredients. Mix well and bake in a greased, 2 in. deep tin in a moderate oven for 40 minutes. This should be served hot and was often used as pudding with a cornflour sauce.

Tewin Apple Cake

In 17th century Hertfordshire farmers and corn masters agreed to help in the parishes with corn at 12 or 18 pence under market price. Hertford County Records show that corn was cheap "by reason no London loaders came down". This old recipe uses bread dough.

1 lb bread dough, well risen	4 oz softened butter
6 oz brown sugar	1 lb cooking apples
1 teaspoon cinnamon	

After the apples have been washed, cored and peeled, chop them finely. Roll out the bread dough about 1/2 inch thick to form a rectangle. Spread with the softened butter, sugar and scattered cinnamon. Press the apple gently into this spice-covered dough and roll it up like a Swiss Roll. Allow it to rest in a warm place for 15 minutes then place in a tin to bake in a hot oven 200 C., 400 F., gas mark 6, for half an hour. The warm apple cake was eaten with cream.

In the churchyard at Tewin is the tomb of Ann Grimston, an atheist who is reported as having uttered a wish, that should there be a God, may a fig tree grow from her heart. Old photographs show what is said to be the very tree growing from Ann's vault where she was placed in 1713. The parish church dates from 1100. Trees grow profusely in Hertfordshire, one photograph from 1913 showing a sycamore tree growing from a tomb at Aldenham near Watford. According to legend in the county, a tree splitting a tomb is a judgement on those who disbelieve the Resurrection.

The photograph of Knebworth House dates from 1897 and shows all its ornate Gothic splendour. On this site has stood the home of the Lytton family since 1490, this building being created by Sir Edward Bulwer Lytton, Victorian statesman and novelist. Charles Dickens participated in amateur theatricals here during a visit in 1850; Queen Elizabeth slept here and certain rooms have for centuries been held to be haunted.

William Hart's Watercress Soup

1 lb watercress	1 1/2 pints white stock
1/2 lb old potatoes	seasoning
1 oz butter	1 oz dripping
1 pint water	slice of old bread

Remove all the leaves from the stalks of the watercress and wash thoroughly. Place in a colander to drain. Peel the potatoes and quarter them, placing in a pan with a pint of cold water. Boil until soft, then drain the potato water into a bowl.

Rub potatoes through a sieve and finely chop the watercress leaves. In the melted butter in a pan, gently cook, but do not brown the watercress. Add to it the sieved potato and the potato water. Stir until all smooth and simmer for 20 minutes. Serve very hot with croutons or sippits.

Mr. Hart, who lived in Letchworth in the 1930s, often saw George Bernard Shaw when he came into the town which was vegetarian-conscious even in those early days.

Mrs. Penrice's Mock Turtle Soup

Coaching dinners amongst rich, young gentlemen were once very popular. In 1872 one coaching club ordered the following for 8 men: "dinner to consist of turtle followed by no other fish but whitebait, followed by grouse, apple fritters and jelly. With the turtle there will be punch, with the whitebait champagne and with the grouse claret, the two former particularly well iced ... there must be cayenne and lemons cut in halves within reach of everyone for the turtle."

the broth and meat from a	seasoning
calf's head	1 bay leaf
sprigs of thyme and marjoram	2 cloves
1 dessertspoon finely chopped	1 onion
parsley	1 oz butter
1 teaspoon lemon juice	1 oz flour

Put 3 pints of the broth into a stewpan with the finely chopped herbs, bay leaf and the onion stuck with cloves. Simmer gently for 2 hours then test and adjust seasoning.

Melt the butter and stir in gradually 1 oz finely sifted flour. Continue to stir until a golden brown colour shows. Add a slice of raw onion, stirring it around after removing pan from fire. Place this thickening in a jar until required. At the end of 2 hours strain the broth and return it to the saucepan, adding the brown thickening to a small quantity and any meat from the calf's head plus the lemon juice. Gradually co-ordinate all the broth and simmer for 5 minutes. Serve very hot. Sometimes forcemeat balls or small dumplings were added 20 minutes before cooking time was up, these being floated on the broth itself.

The photograph of the school room at Royston's Home for little girls must date from the early days of the century. Charity uniforms, strict discipline, old gas-lighting and desks would no doubt go along with dreary, monotonous diet sheets, In the days of stagecoaches Roystia's Cross, as Royston was once known, was on the route between London and Edinburgh, a part of Ermine Street. The Corn Exchange of 1829 led to the removal of the market, a busy place for food.

Bushey Bread

At Bushey, from the days of Queen Anne, on a flat tomb in the churchyard,
each Sunday morning 12 loaves of bread were set, for 12 poor people, the gift of Dame Fuller who had also endowed the Free School at Watford. A bread recipe from Bushey obtained 30 years ago was therefore appropriate.

This wholemeal dough makes 2 loaves or 20 rolls.

1 1/2 lb wholemeal flour	3/4 pint tepid water
1 oz lard	1 teaspoon salt
1 oz fresh yeast	

Mix the flour with the salt and rub in the lard with fingertips, lifting the mixture to get air into it. Crumble the yeast in warm water and stir well. Pour the yeast liquid and mix into the flour with the hands drawing the dough together. If extra water is needed, add it carefully, a little at a time. Flour varies in absorbency. After turning the dough onto a floured board, knead it well for 10 minutes. Cover with a mixing bowl and leave to rest. Preheat oven to Hot 230 C., 450 F. After 10 minutes divide the dough into two portions and place in greased tins. Put the tins in a warm place and cover with a clean, damp cloth. When the dough has almost doubled in size, glaze with weak milk and sprinkle oatmeal on top.

Bake loaves for 40 minutes until well risen. Rolls take only 20 minutes. To test if ready, tap the base of the loaf. It should sound hollow.

Old-Time Gingerbread

1 lb flour	1/2 teaspoon bicarb of soda
6 oz margarine (bacon dripping was used in the original recipe)	4 tablespoons black treacle
	4 oz sugar
2 oz almonds	2 oz candied peel
1 oz ground ginger	1 teaspoon mixed spice
	1 egg

Chop the almonds and candied peel. Mix with ginger, spice and flour. Warm the treacle, margarine and sugar together, beating well. Add the egg then dissolve the soda in a little lukewarm milk. Mix all well together and bake in a slow oven for 2 hours without disturbing.

At St. Alban's the huge, triangular open space from Chequer Street to French Row was gradually filled in after the Norman Conquest. Shambles means a stall, and there were shambles of flesh, fish, leather and pudding sellers. The stalls became permanent shops by the 14th century, French Row having once been Cobblers' Row. Malt, wheat and wool markets were held. The evolution of the inn from the village ale house came about in 1543 when a law ordered "that all who sell ale, bread and other victuals shall put a sign in front of their door, and further that they shall provide honest service and hospitality." The Fighting Cocks at St. Alban's is one of many examples.

Baldock Doughnuts

These were eaten only on Ash Wednesdays.

1/2 oz yeast
1 teaspoon caster sugar

1/4 lb flour
1 1/2 gills warm milk

For the dough

3/4 lb flour
2 oz melted butter
raspberry jam

2 oz caster sugar
2 eggs

Cream the yeast and sugar for one minute till liquid. Add milk and strain into the flour. Beat well. Cover with cloth and leave to rise in a warm place for an hour. To make the dough, mix the flour and sugar in a large basin and make a hollow in the centre. Beat the eggs and melt the butter and put them in the hollow with the mixture that has been rising. Mix and beat, putting again in a warm place, covered with a cloth for 1 1/2 hours. Divide the dough into small, round pieces, placing a spoonful of jam in each and drawing the dough over it. A large, old-fashioned kettle of deep fat was used to cook the doughnuts for 15 minutes. Drain and roll in caster sugar.

Queen Eleanor, wife of King Edward I, died in Lincolnshire in 1290. It took 13 days for her funeral procession to reach Westminster Abbey and at every spot where her body rested on the journey Edward vowed to raise a cross. Only three now remain. This at Waltham Cross was photographed in the 1930s.

Fig Jelly

Palm Sunday in Hertfordshire, as in Sussex, was associated with boiled fig pudding or fig jelly. As late as the 1950s at Northaw Stores customers still requested their figs for Fig Sunday and Welwyn Stores sold figs and rice as a special offer, the rice being made into a creamy pudding to be eaten with the stewed, cut-up figs. Mrs. E.M. Smith of Digswell recalled the grocers asking: "Have you bought for Fig Sunday?" The puddings there were "boiled suet with fig filling". Mrs. Mary Coburn of Harpenden and Mrs. K. L. Allen of Welwyn Garden City recalled this custom well. Spiced buns also were given out to babies on Good Friday, hopefully conferring life-long good fortune.

The fig jelly was made by stewing 1 lb figs with 4 oz sugar and straining off the juice. One leaf of melted gelatine added and well stirred made a delicious fig jelly.

This is a special train pulled by "Wellington", a contractor's engine, at Chesham on the opening day of the extension of the railway from Rickmansworth, July 8th. 1889. Note the large crowd on the bank overlooking the line. John Dickinson, the paper manufacturer, as his business grew, built Croxley Mills in Rickmansworth in 1828. The firm introduced silk- thread as protection against forgery and along with other paper mills used the River Gade in the process. The canal also played a big part in the success of this firm famous today for Basildon Bond.

Tring Dumplings

Just as Cornish pasties with meat at one end and fruit or jam at the other were carried down tin mines, so were Tring dumplings taken into the fields by Hertfordshire agricultural labourers and consumed for "bever" or mid-morning snack. Percy B. Birtchnell, native of Hertfordshire, said: "This dumpling depended for its success upon a sound inter-departmental wall," presumably so that the sweet and savoury twain never met. One housewife left a protruding piece of straw or "plait" to indicate the meat end for her good man. Again, specifics were missing but this intriguing dumpling had to be tried out. Suet, universally once a great filler taking the edge off appetite, figured widely in every county we visited.

Make the suet pastry by mixing 4 oz grated beef suet, 1/2 lb flour, 3 oz breadcrumbs and binding with a little cold water to form a soft dough. Roll out and cut pastry into individual pieces about 6 inches square. Raise a middle "wall". Fill on either side using chopped pork or bacon one end, chopped sugary apple at the other, crimping edges of pastry together. The dumplings were traditionally boiled in a clean cloth.

Even if the two-way system breaks down it still tastes good! It was of Tring's Rose and Crown that Cobbett said: "Had the best public dinner I ever saw." He was guest of honour for seven hours, at a time in the county's history when roasted rye was used in place of coffee, the latter beverage being so expensive. The notorious highwaywoman Katherine Ferrers was ranging Nomansland Common when "sheep's windpipe with turnip tops" was a Hertfordshire dish, a recipe I did not feel inclined to seek.

The Ancient British Causeway at St. Alban's is said to be the road down which Alban was hurried to his death. A ruling prince and pagan, Alban became influenced by Christian preaching, harbouring and protecting a Christian priest in his house. Subsequently Alban was condemned to be beheaded as he refused to perform any more pagan sacrifices. A miracle occurred on the way to the scene of his martyrdom on a hill half a mile from the Roman city of Verulamium, described by the Venerable Bede as being "beautifully garnished with divers herbs and flowers". Alban was the first man in Britain to die for his faith.

Swimmers

Left-over portions of the suet pastry about the size of a walnut were "dobbed into the boiling pot" and know as "swimmers". As they rose to the surface the dumplings were lifted out with a large, slatted spoon and eaten straight from the pot very hot with honey, jam or treacle: well remembered by Mr. Charlie Ayre who could not recall the recipe for Baldock doughnuts other than that these were small, spiced, golden brown and also eaten hot. "Nothing seemed nicer."

Walnut Pudding

This recipe is 101 years old and is very precise about the walnuts - 14 - which you "Shell and Peel". (A packet of shelled walnuts will be more convenient these days.) It was popular in Autumn and at Christmas time when the nuts ripened. It seems to have been popular also at the hill station, Simla India.

14 walnuts (28 if using packet halved nuts)	3 oz breadcrumbs
	3/4 teaspoon vanilla
1 teacup full of milk	2 eggs
	4 oz sugar

Put the shelled nuts in a pan with the milk and breadcrumbs and allow to come to the boil, then simmer gently for a few minutes. Take from the fire and allow to cool. Add sugar, yolks of eggs and vanilla. Pour the mixture into a well-buttered pie dish and bake in a moderate oven for 1/2 hour. Beat the whites of the eggs very stiffly and pile on the top of the pudding. No mentioned is made of browning the topping but many will be tempted to place under the grill for a few minutes for this purpose.

Cucumber Cream Soup

1 cucumber	1 cup shelled peas
12 chives	1 carrot
2 oz butter	1/2 gill cream
3 pints stock	2 oz flour
salt, pepper, grated nutmeg	

Wash & cut unpeeled cucumber in half lengthwise and scrape out seeds. Wash and scrape the carrot. Dice the vegetables and cucumber and snip the chives into small pieces. Boil the stock and put in carrot and cucumber. Boil for 10 minutes and add peas and chives. When the vegetables are tender pour the soup into a basin. Melt the butter in the same saucepan, stir in flour and gradually add the soup. Stir until it boils and boil for 5 minutes. Season with the salt, pepper and nutmeg. Remove soup from heat and when it has cooled a little add the cream. Stir well and pour into a tureen.

Sweet Sauce if there be no cream

1 pint new milk	rind of lemon
3 yolks of eggs	a little sugar

Put the milk into a pan with the rind of lemon and let it come to boiling point. Strain over the well-beaten yolks. Pour back and stir but do not let it boil. Sweeten to taste.

Simple Sauce

1 teaspoon butter	a little nutmeg
1 breakfast cup of milk and water	1 dessertspoon cornflour
	1 dessertspoon brown sugar

Mix all smoothly together and stir until it boils. Cook on for a few minutes, continually stirring for smoothness sake.

Seville Orange Marmalade

6 Seville oranges	2 lemons
6 lb preserving sugar	4 pints water

Scrub the fruit to ensure cleanliness. Cut each orange into two and squeeze out juices. Place these shells of fruit into a large earthenware bowl and cover with the water. Soak for at least a whole day with a muslin bag of the fruit pips suspended in the water. Next day, simmer these skins for 2 hours in the preserving pan. Rough cut or shred finely as desired, the cooled skins. Return the muslin bag of pips to the pan and boil all up again with the fruit juices and the sugar, dissolving this gradually. The pips in the muslin bag are important as they add flavour and aid the set. After the sugar and juice have been added it should be necessary to boil rapidly for only 15 minutes. Test for set, then put in warm, clean jars and seal at once.

To Boil a Hare in a Jug

1 hare	1 chopped onion
1 faggot of herbs	2 oz butter
1 pint cider	seasoning

Soak the hare. Cut into pieces. A seasoning of grated nutmeg, salt and pepper is used to sprinkle over the joints. Brown the meat in butter then place all in a tall, earthenware crock with a faggot of herbs and a chopped Spanish onion. Put the crock in a big saucepan of water. Pour in the cider and seal the pot well. Simmer for 3 hours, adding water to the pan as necessary.

"Licence for free warren" was the right to hunt hares, rabbits, partridges and pheasants at such places as Sawbridgeworth. Of three great parks in Hunsdon the Old Park was in existence by 1124. The Normans introduced coney beds protecting rabbits, to provide them with fresh meat in winter. By the 16th century the bulk of Crown land in Hertfordshire had gone to people with Court connections like Lord Chancellor, Sir Thomas Audley.

Potato and Cheese Cakes

10 oz cooked mashed potato	1 teaspoon ground sea salt
1 level teaspoon dry mustard	1 egg well beaten
4 oz finely grated cheese	

Mix all the ingredients well together. On a greased griddle or the base of a thick frying pan press small, rounded quantities of this mixture. Cook over gentle heat, turning to brown the other side or these potato and cheese cakes can be baked on a greased baking sheet in the oven at 200 C., 400 F., gas mark 6, for 15 minutes.

Tipsy Trifle

8 trifle sponges	and plum jam
2 level tablespoons each of	2 tablespoons brandy
home made strawberry jam	1 oz flaked almonds
1 pint milk	jelly
6 egg yolks	6 tablespoons sherry
toasted almonds	1/4 pint thick cream
ratafia biscuits	3 level tablespoons caster
2 level tablespoons orange	sugar

Sandwich the split-open sponges with the jams and jelly. Put in sufficient ratafia biscuits to cover base of a large, glass trifle dish and sprinkle with the brandy. Arrange half the sponges on top of the ratafias, sprinkle with sherry and almonds. Arrange the other half of the sponges on top with the rest of the almonds and sherry. Press down lightly. Heat the milk and cream in a saucepan.

Beat egg yolks and sugar together. Pour the heated milk and cream over them and cook in a double boiler until the resulting custard coats the back of a wooden spoon. When it has cooled, pour over the sponges in the trifle bowl and allow to rest all night. Decorate with toasted almonds and angelica next day. It does not really need any more cream, but some people indulge, especially at Christmas tea.

Partridge Soup

Skin 2 partridges and cut into pieces with 4 slices of ham, a stick of celery and 3 large, sliced onions. Fry all in butter till brown. Put into a stew pan with 5 parts of water, a few peppercorns and a shank of mutton. Stew gently for 2 hours then strain through a sieve. Put it back into stew pan and when really hot pour into a tureen to serve.

Ox Cheek

Boil 4 lb ox head for 2 hours. Take the meat off the bones and lay the pieces in a mould. Press down. Strain the liquor in which the head was boiled. Season with pepper and salt and a spoon of ketchup if liked. Place the mould in the oven and bake for one hour, having well moistened the meat in the mould with the liquor. What is left of this can later be reduced in content, thickened with a little flour and served with the mould, if eaten hot.

Vegetable Soup

5 cucumbers	5 lettuce hearts
2 sprigs of mint	3 small onions
pepper and salt	1 lb young peas
small quantity of parsley	

"The first two items, cucumbers and lettuce hearts should be pared and sliced, then place all into a saucepan with 1/2 lb fresh butter and stew gently for half an hour. Then pour 2 quarts of boiling water onto the vegetables and stew for 2 hours. Before serving add a little flour and water to thicken. Very small dumplings boiled in water were served with this early Victorian soup."

This unusual photograph shows a 22 ton barge being hauled through Hertfordshire in the 1930s, probably bound for the Grand Union Canal. It is passing the George and Dragon Inn owned by Trust Houses Ltd. The Duke of Bridgwater, associated with canal building, constructed none in Hertfordshire but it was his home. The important canal is the Grand Union Canal which joined the Thames with the Midland Canal system. Coal was transported and manure for the farms.

Chipping Barnet Chocolate Souffle

1 oz butter	1/2 oz flour
1 oz unsweetened grated	1 gill milk
chocolate	2 oz sugar
2 tablespoons hot water	3 eggs
1/2 teaspoon vanilla	

Melt the butter, add the flour and stir in the milk. Melt the chocolate on top of a double saucepan. Add sugar and hot water and combine with the sauce just made. Add the yolks of eggs, well beaten, fold in the whites beaten until stiff and dry. Flavour with vanilla and bake in a buttered souffle dish in a moderate oven at 150 C. for 30-45 minutes.

Serve the chocolate souffle with a foamy sauce made as follows:

1 oz butter	1/2 oz flour
4 oz sugar	1 gill water
1 teaspoon vanilla	1 egg

Cream the butter, add the flour and sugar gradually, stirring constantly. Add the egg yolk, well beaten, the water and the vanilla. Cook in a double boiler until the mixture thickens, stirring constantly. Cool, then add the stiffly-beaten egg white just before serving.

Turkish Delight

an Edwardian recipe dated 1907 from Potter's Bar

"Soak 1 oz of very good gelatine in half a pint of cold water. Put into a saucepan with 2 lb of loaf sugar and when it boils stir for 20 minutes. Take the mixture off the fire and add 2 teaspoons of vanilla essence and one teaspoon of essence of lemon. Pour into wet soup plates. Stand for 2 hours and then cut in squares and cover with icing sugar."

Oatmeal Biscuits

6 oz lard	8 oz brown sugar
1 egg	2 fl oz water
1 teaspoon vanilla essence	12 oz oats
4 oz plain flour	1/2 teaspoon bicarb of soda

Heat oven to 180 C. Beat together the lard, sugar, egg, water and vanilla. Cream it well then add remaining ingredients. Grease a baking sheet and drop the mixture in teaspoons onto it. Bake for 20 minutes.

Grain in pagan times was stored in pits dug in the chalk, the grain being part-roasted to prevent germination. Later came an improvement for Hertfordshire villages in the shape of earthenware jars which came from the area later known as Belgium.

Pork Pie

On a postcard from the Museum at Tring, August 1910, Lilly wrote to Ena, "I will come over on my bike. Hope you will be able to get a decent machine. The jellied pork pie will be fine for the ride."

For the pastry

1 lb flour, 1 oz butter, 3 oz lard, water

For the filling

1 1/2 lb lean pork, 1 teaspoon chopped fresh sage, beaten egg. Into the sifted flour should be gently poured the hot melted fats in 1 1/2 gills of water. (Add the fat, cut into flakes, gradually to the water and bring to the boil.) Knead the stiff paste very well. If difficult to mould, add a little more hot water.

Line the bottom and sides of a pork pie mould or cake tin, with the paste, leaving enough for the pie lid, but be sure to keep that warm. Fill the moulds with tightly-packed pork cut into small pieces. Season. Scatter on the sage between layers. Put on the pastry lid, decorating with pastry leaves if desired. Brush with beaten egg. Make a hole in the top and bake in a slow oven for 2 1/2 hours.

When it is cold, aspic jelly or jelly from pork bones boiled in water should be carefully funnelled in through the hole in the pork pie lid and allowed to cool on a marble slab.

Prune Puff

4 eggs   1/2 cup powdered sugar
1 cup cooked prunes

Whip the egg whites to a stiff froth. Add sugar slowly, still beating. Add the stoned, chopped prunes. Bake in a pudding dish in a moderate oven for 10 minutes. Serve cold with egg custard, using the egg yolks.

In summer soft fruits were used in the same way but usually cream or ice cream accompanied the fruit puff.

When my friend Pamela first went to live in Harpenden thirty years ago, settling in the evocatively named Ox Lane, she sent back to Lancashire the following recipe. Pam, famous in the north for her Scotch Eggs had discovered:

Sausage and Egg Pie

6 oz plain flour   6 oz sausage meat
2 hard-boiled eggs   3 oz lard
2 tomatoes

First make the shortcrust pastry by rubbing the lard lightly into the flour. Line a flan tin with the pastry. Smooth the sausage meat all over the bottom of the tin. Slice the ripe tomatoes very thinly and layer over the sausage meat. Slice the eggs thinly and place on top of the tomatoes. Make a pastry lid for the pie and place on top. Bake in a hot oven for 15 minutes at 210 C. then turn down to 180 C. for another 1/2 hour or a little longer if it needs browning more.

This pie can be served hot or cold, the latter way with salad, but we liked to eat it hot for family tea on cold winter nights.

Implement Gate, New Mill, Tring.

The agricultural nature of the county is expressed in this 1906 photograph of an Implement Gate at New Mill, Tring, which uses spades, a scythe, sickles, billhook etc. in its construction. Before the introduction of carborundum, sharpening stones or strickles were used to whet tools. Sharpening a scythe was an art, tar or sand being used, but a good scyther could cut three acres a day by hand, although most found the sickle easier to handle.

Royston Rich Cake

8 oz butter	2 oz blanched, chopped
8 oz soft brown sugar	almonds
1 tablespoon treacle	3 oz mixed chopped peel
5 large eggs	4 oz glace cherries
9 oz plain flour	6 oz sultanas
1 teaspoon mixed spice	6 oz raisins
1/2 teaspoon grated nutmeg	10 oz currants
grated rind of 1 orange	grated rind of 1 lemon

Pre-heat oven to 150 C. and grease and line a deep 9 inch round cake tin. Cream butter, sugar and treacle. Beat in eggs one at a time, adding a tablespoon of the flour with the last two. Sieve in remaining flour and spices. Stir in nuts, the cleaned, dried fruit and lemon and orange rind. Turn the mixture into a prepared tin and smooth the top, hollowing slightly. Bake at 150 C., 300 F., gas mark 2 for 3-4 hours.

The old-fashioned sugar, butter method has long been used for making rich fruit cakes. Oranges and lemons were traditionally added to give a distinct flavour, the citrus flavour being complemented by the sweetness of marzipan and icing sugar.

If icing is to be done, coat the cake with boiling apricot jam and leave it to dry for a week. Sprinkle 2 tablespoons of rum over the base of the cake before icing it.

For broilering or brandering, one old Hertfordshire cookery book recommends: "have a gridiron or brander very clean and the fire very clear and bright, but not too strong; a little salt sprinkled over the fire will keep down the flame. A fork should never be put into flesh while cooking." This was to prevent juices escaping. The aim was to seal in all the juices and retain full flavour, but without any charring.

1893 Plain Cookery and Laundry Work recipes for use in Elementary Schools in classes for technical instruction, price one penny, lays stress on invalid cookery, listing Invalid Custard, Lemonade, Rhubarb Water, Apple Water, Linseed Tea, Stewed Beef and Rice Mould. Examples of simple recipes are: Stewed Rabbit, Oatmeal Biscuits, and Poor Man's Goose, made from "scraps of pork, onions, flour and sage".

Steamed Fig Pudding

When summer fruits were not available especially in the months after Christmas and when all bottled fruit had been used, dried figs, prunes and apricots appeared in puddings, the fruit being washed and soaked overnight.

1/4 cup margarine	1 cup sugar
1 cup milk	1 egg
2 cups flour	4 teaspoons baking powder
1 spoonful fresh lemon juice	2 cups chopped figs

Cream margarine and sugar. Add beaten egg and milk and mix well. Sift the flour and baking powder into the mixture then add lemon juice and figs. After mixing well together pour into a well-greased pudding basin which allows an inch for the mixture to rise. Steam for 2 hours and serve with a sweet sauce.

Hitchin Corn Exchange in 1917 was one example of its kind in a county famed for corn and the furtherance of agriculture. John Bennet Lawes on his Rothamsted estate laid the foundation of scientific agriculture. In one field wheat has grown continuously since 1843, the centre at Rothamsted undoubtedly increasing the world's bread supply. Lawes set up a factory for the production of fertilisers and was interested in soil improvement and cattle feeds, which he developed on revolutionary lines. The photograph shows the typical lay-out of a sample corn market.

Apple Charlotte

Named after Queen Charlotte, wife of George 111, this delicious old pudding, still eaten in Hertfordshire, needs to be made with generous proportions of butter and fruit.

1 1/2 lb cooking apples	6 oz unsalted butter
2 egg yolks	1/2 real home-baked bread gone stale

Wash, peel and cut up the apples. Cook them gently in a thin layer of water at the bottom of a heavy pan to which has been added a knob of butter. Cook to a puree, adding sugar to taste. When mixture has cooled, add the egg yolks, well whisked.

Cut the butter into cubes and melt in a pan until it becomes a yellow oil. Coat the Charlotte tin with some of this. The bread should be free of crusts and cut into neat slices for lining the Charlotte tin - one big slice for the bottom. All slices are dipped in the butter, leaving no gaps between slices. Fill with the apple puree. Make a lid of bread also dipped in butter and melted. Bake for one hour, first at 200 C. for 20 minutes, then at 190 C. until browned and crisp. It should be served with cream, but we found an egg custard is delicious with this Charlotte, fit for a queen.

For centuries produce was sold around the Market Cross at Hitchin, men and women arriving very early with baskets containing butter, eggs, apples, mushrooms, walnuts, watercress, elderberries, blackberries, bundles of herbs, young pigeons, fowl or whatever was in season.

Bishops Stortford Town Council bought the house in which Cecil Rhodes was born and the house next door, to turn into a museum in honour of Rhodes, empire builder after whom Rhodesia was named. This photograph dates from the 1950s. One of eleven children, he was a son of the vicar of St. Michaels's. Other famous people born in Hertfordshire are Sir Henry Bessemer, William Cowper, George Chapman and Thomas Campion.

Wood Pigeon Pie

This was served with watercress and Hertfordshire tracklements

2 wood pigeons	6 slices bacon, all fat removed
3/4 lb best quality steak	1 large, well-chopped onion

After cutting up the steak, put in a pan with the chopped onion, a little pepper and 1/2 teaspoon of herbs. Cover with water and simmer for one hour.

Place the prepared pigeon breasts in a pie dish with the steak and cut-up bacon, layering these ingredients. Half fill with the steak stock. Make a shortcrust pastry lid for the pie and bake in a hot oven until the pastry is brown, then turn oven temperature to low for a further half hour. The remainder of the stock can be boiled down to form a concentrate and poured carefully through the hole in the pie lid. It forms a delicate jelly in the pigeon pie when quite cold.

The Illustrated London News of November 22nd 1879 showed James Bower, the first Conductor, of a Great Northern Railway Pullman Dining Car, "Prince of Wales", serving customers at separate tables covered with snowy, damask cloths. The chef was James Oswin and assisted by his son they prepared mock turtle soup, lobster mayonnaise, mutton cutlets, roast beef, green peas, mashed potatoes, a dessert and cheese and celery.

The Flying Scotsman, which first ran in June 1862, by the 1930s had an all-electric kitchen, serving meals for travellers as the train hurtled past Stevenage and Hitchin. In 1945 I was commuting regularly on the Mancunian and well remember some excellent soups issuing from the galley. Travelling at speeds of over 70 m.p.h., it was unusual for a drop to be spilled, and the waiters' dexterity with coffee pots, part of gleaming silver service was equally to be admired.

Tomato Soup

1 medium onion thinly sliced
2 rashers bacon, cut up and rind removed
1 carrot cut up fine
bouquet garni
1 oz plain flour
sea salt and ground black pepper
2 oz butter

1 1/2 pints vegetable stock
1 lb tomatoes roughly chopped
1 stick of celery cut up fine
1 teaspoon sugar
1/2 pint milk
chopped chives

Melt half the butter. Sweat bacon and onion until onion is soft but not browned. Add the stock and the vegetables, bouquet garni and sugar. Bring to boil slowly and simmer for one hour. Take out bouquet garni and liquidise. Blend remaining half of butter with the flour and milk. Whisk this in. Reheat the tomato soup. Season. Serve hot with a swirl of cream and, centre-placed, teaspoon of freshly chopped chives. Croutons if desired.

This magnificent Norman doorway in the south transept of the Cathedral of St. Alban's was photographed in 1918. Rich in Norman work, in addition to the tower and transepts much of the Abbey Church still exists. The Normans rebuilt Offa's Benedictine Abbey, founded in 793 soon after they arrived. It is said that King Offa found Alban's bones and placed them in the Abbey Church, where can be seen a magnificent tomb in memory of the martyr.

Puckeridge Farm Bread

1 cup washed sultanas (these are soaked in tea all night) Add 1 beaten egg, 2 teacups of self raising flour and a cup of Demerara sugar.

Mix well and pour into an oblong, greased tin. Bake at 180 C. for 30 minutes.

It was eaten hot with butter.

Tripe and Onions from Berkhamsted

Wash tripe and cut into small pieces 2 inches long. Put in a large frying pan with plenty of sliced onions. Add seasoned milk and cook until tender over gentle heat. Serve with boiled potatoes.

James Selby, the best known of all professional coachmen, in 1870 was driving the St. Alban's coach in winter. He later joined Mr. Cowland to form a coachbuilding firm and a light coach was made especially for his use. The service established between London's White Horse Cellar and St. Alban's lasted eleven years, running in all weathers. In 1881 when he arrived in a snowstorm, his hat was frozen to his head and could be released only by pouring hot water upon it.

Saffron Cake

This was a great favourite at one time. Cambridgeshire grew fields full of purple crocus to supply saffron, obtainable from the stamens of the flower, but over the border in Hertfordshire the crop was grown in small closes, protected by wattle fences. This interfered less with the rotation of crops in larger field systems.

2 lb flour	pinch of salt
2 oz candied peel	1 lb butter
1 lb currants	4 oz sugar
1/2 dram saffron	1 oz yeast in a little warm milk with sugar

Cut up the saffron and soak it overnight in boiling water. Rub the butter in the flour. Add sugar, salt, peel and currants. Add the yeast and milk, pouring it into the centre of the flour mixture. Mix by hand into a dough, adding extra milk and the saffron water. Leave in a warm place to rise for some time then bake in a tin for an hour at 180 C.

A 200 year old remedy for stomach pain uses a sprinkle of saffron upon 2 baked Seville oranges, steeped overnight in 2 pints of wine, the oranges cut up. The liquid procured after straining next day was drunk to relieve the pain.

Lamb and Chestnuts

1 shoulder of lamb	1/2 pint stock
1 oz butter	8 oz chestnuts
1 tablespoon chopped lemon and thyme	1 large sliced onion
	1 tablespoon chopped marjoram

The lamb should be boned and the meat cut into pieces.

Skin the chestnuts. Melt the butter in a heavy pan. Brown the lamb in this.Lower heat and put in the onion to soften it. Stir in the chestnuts and pour in the stock. Bring slowly to the boil. Add the thyme and marjoram and replace the lamb. Cover the pan and leave on low heat for 35 minutes.

Acknowledgements

I should like to thank:

Nellie Bateson
Miss Janice Brooker
Mr. E.M. Broome, O.B.E.
Mr. Stanley Butterworth
Mrs. Barbara Cartland, D. St. J.
Mr. Doug Forton
Nigel Gordon
Great Bradwins Apiaries
William R. Hart
Hertfordshire County Library
Hertfordshire Federation of Women's
Institutes
Katherine Howell
Ann C. Kenny
Mrs. S. Penrice
Mr. J.C. Plummer
Public Libraries: Hertford,
Rickmansworth, St. Alban's, Ware,
Watford, Welwyn
Red Rose Postcard Club

Regina Royal Jelly Ltd.
Alison Robertson
Ron Severs
Mrs. G. Shaw
Mr. Jack Stasiak
Mrs. R. Stein
Miss Marian Stott
Brian V. Sweet
Tourist Information Centres:
Berkhamsted, Bishop's Stortford, Hemel
Hempstead, Hertford, St. Alban's,
Stevenage, Welwyn Garden City
Vintage Postcards International
Annie Ward
Pamela Weatherley
Ida Brodersen
Heather Fitzsimmons
"Hertfordshire Countryside"
P.C. Birtchnell.